Theatre Diary

D1744310

Name: _____

Address: _____

_____

_____

Phone: _____

Year: _____

Cover painting: Bal de l'Opéra (Ball at the Opera)
By Eugène Charles François Guérard, 1821–1866

Copyright 2015

Theatre Diary		
Theatrical Production	Date	Page

Theatre Diary		
Theatrical Production	Date	Page

Theatre Diary		
Theatrical Production	Date	Page

Theatre Diary		
Theatrical Production	Date	Page

Theatre Diary		
Theatrical Production	Date	Page

Title

Year

Director

Producer

Writer/s

Actors

Reaction/Review/ Plot/Quotes/

Who I saw it with:

Cost:

£

Theatre

☆ ☆ ☆ ☆ ☆

Title   Year

Director   Producer

Writer/s

Actors

Reaction/Review/ Plot/Quotes/

Who I saw it with: Cost:

                                                               £

Theatre

☆ ☆ ☆ ☆ ☆

Title

Year

Director

Producer

Writer/s

Actors

Reaction/Review/ Plot/Quotes/

Who I saw it with:

Cost:

£

Theatre

☆ ☆ ☆ ☆ ☆

Title

Year

Director

Producer

Writer/s

Actors

Reaction/Review/ Plot/Quotes/

Who I saw it with:

Cost:

£

Theatre

☆ ☆ ☆ ☆ ☆

Title

Year

Director

Producer

Writer/s

Actors

Reaction/Review/ Plot/Quotes/

Who I saw it with:

Cost:

£

Theatre

☆ ☆ ☆ ☆ ☆

Title

Year

Director

Producer

Writer/s

Actors

Reaction/Review/ Plot/Quotes/

Who I saw it with:

Cost:

£

Theatre

☆ ☆ ☆ ☆ ☆

Title

Year

Director

Producer

Writer/s

Actors

Reaction/Review/ Plot/Quotes/

Who I saw it with:

Cost:

£

Theatre

☆ ☆ ☆ ☆ ☆

Title

Year

Director

Producer

Writer/s

Actors

Reaction/Review/ Plot/Quotes/

Who I saw it with:

Cost:

£

Theatre

☆ ☆ ☆ ☆ ☆

Title

Year

Director

Producer

Writer/s

Actors

Reaction/Review/ Plot/Quotes/

Who I saw it with:

Cost:

£

Theatre

☆ ☆ ☆ ☆ ☆

Title

Year

Director

Producer

Writer/s

Actors

Reaction/Review/ Plot/Quotes/

Who I saw it with:

Cost:

£

Theatre

☆ ☆ ☆ ☆ ☆

Title

Year

Director

Producer

Writer/s

Actors

Reaction/Review/ Plot/Quotes/

Who I saw it with:

Cost:

£

Theatre

☆ ☆ ☆ ☆ ☆

Title

Year

Director

Producer

Writer/s

Actors

Reaction/Review/ Plot/Quotes/

Who I saw it with:

Cost:

£

Theatre

☆ ☆ ☆ ☆ ☆

Title _____ Year _____

Director _____ Producer _____

Writer/s _____

Actors _____

Reaction/Review/ Plot/Quotes/ _____

Who I saw it with: _____ Cost:

£ _____

Theatre _____

☆ ☆ ☆ ☆ ☆

Title

Year

Director

Producer

Writer/s

Actors

Reaction/Review/ Plot/Quotes/

Who I saw it with:

Cost:

£

Theatre

☆ ☆ ☆ ☆ ☆

Title   Year

Director   Producer

Writer/s

Actors

Reaction/Review/ Plot/Quotes/

Who 9 saw it with: Cost:

                                                                             £

Theatre

☆ ☆ ☆ ☆ ☆

Title   Year

Director   Producer

Writer/s

Actors

Reaction/Review/ Plot/Quotes/

Who I saw it with: Cost:

                                                   £

Theatre

☆ ☆ ☆ ☆ ☆

Title

Year

Director

Producer

Writer/s

Actors

Reaction/Review/ Plot/Quotes/

Who I saw it with:

Cost:

£

Theatre

☆ ☆ ☆ ☆ ☆

Title   Year

Director   Producer

Writer/s

Actors

Reaction/Review/ Plot/Quotes/

Who I saw it with: Cost:

                                                              £

Theatre

☆ ☆ ☆ ☆ ☆

Title   Year

Director   Producer

Writer/s

Actors

Reaction/Review/ Plot/Quotes/

Who I saw it with: Cost:

£

Theatre

☆ ☆ ☆ ☆ ☆

Title

Year

Director

Producer

Writer/s

Actors

Reaction/Review/ Plot/Quotes/

Who I saw it with:

Cost:

£

Theatre

☆ ☆ ☆ ☆ ☆

Title

Year

Director

Producer

Writer/s

Actors

Reaction/Review/ Plot/Quotes/

Who I saw it with:

Cost:

£

Theatre

☆ ☆ ☆ ☆ ☆

Title

Year

Director

Producer

Writer/s

Actors

Reaction/Review/ Plot/Quotes/

Who I saw it with:

Cost:

£

Theatre

☆ ☆ ☆ ☆ ☆

Title   Year

Director   Producer

Writer/s

Actors

Reaction/Review/ Plot/Quotes/

Who I saw it with: Cost:

£

Theatre

☆ ☆ ☆ ☆ ☆

Title

Year

Director

Producer

Writer/s

Actors

Reaction/Review/ Plot/Quotes/

Who I saw it with:

Cost:

£

Theatre

☆ ☆ ☆ ☆ ☆

Title   Year

Director   Producer

Writer/s

Actors

Reaction/Review/ Plot/Quotes/

Who I saw it with: Cost:

£

Theatre

☆ ☆ ☆ ☆ ☆

Title   Year

Director   Producer

Writer/s

Actors

Reaction/Review/ Plot/Quotes/

Who 9 saw it with: Cost:

£

Theatre

☆ ☆ ☆ ☆ ☆

Title   Year

Director   Producer

Writer/s

Actors

Reaction/Review/ Plot/Quotes/

Who I saw it with: Cost:

                                                         £

Theatre

☆ ☆ ☆ ☆ ☆

Title

Year

Director

Producer

Writer/s

Actors

Reaction/Review/ Plot/Quotes/

Who I saw it with:

Cost:

£

Theatre

☆ ☆ ☆ ☆ ☆

Title   Year

Director   Producer

Writer/s

Actors

Reaction/Review/ Plot/Quotes/

Who I saw it with: Cost:

                                                              £

Theatre

☆ ☆ ☆ ☆ ☆

Title   Year

Director   Producer

Writer/s

Actors

Reaction/Review/ Plot/Quotes/

Who I saw it with: Cost:

£

Theatre

☆ ☆ ☆ ☆ ☆

Title   Year

Director   Producer

Writer/s

Actors

Reaction/Review/ Plot/Quotes/

Who I saw it with: Cost:

£

Theatre

☆ ☆ ☆ ☆ ☆

Title   Year

Director   Producer

Writer/s

Actors

Reaction/Review/ Plot/Quotes/

Who I saw it with: Cost:

£

Theatre

☆ ☆ ☆ ☆ ☆

Title

Year

Director

Producer

Writer/s

Actors

Reaction/Review/ Plot/Quotes/

Who I saw it with:

Cost:

£

Theatre

☆ ☆ ☆ ☆ ☆

Title

Year

Director

Producer

Writer/s

Actors

Reaction/Review/ Plot/Quotes/

Who I saw it with:

Cost:

£

Theatre

☆ ☆ ☆ ☆ ☆

Title   Year

Director   Producer

Writer/s

Actors

Reaction/Review/ Plot/Quotes/

Who I saw it with: Cost:

£

Theatre

☆ ☆ ☆ ☆ ☆

Title

Year

Director

Producer

Writer/s

Actors

Reaction/Review/ Plot/Quotes/

Who 9 saw it with:

Cost:

£

Theatre

☆ ☆ ☆ ☆ ☆

Title

Year

Director

Producer

Writer/s

Actors

Reaction/Review/ Plot/Quotes/

Who I saw it with:

Cost:

£

Theatre

☆ ☆ ☆ ☆ ☆

Title

Year

Director

Producer

Writer/s

Actors

Reaction/Review/ Plot/Quotes/

Who I saw it with:

Cost:

£

Theatre

☆ ☆ ☆ ☆ ☆

Title

Year

Director

Producer

Writer/s

Actors

Reaction/Review/ Plot/Quotes/

Who I saw it with:

Cost:

£

Theatre

☆☆☆☆☆

Title   Year

Director   Producer

Writer/s

Actors

Reaction/Review/ Plot/Quotes/

Who I saw it with: Cost:

                                                         £

Theatre

☆ ☆ ☆ ☆ ☆

Title   Year

Director   Producer

Writer/s

Actors

Reaction/Review/ Plot/Quotes/

Who I saw it with: Cost:

                                               £

Theatre

☆ ☆ ☆ ☆ ☆

Title   Year

Director   Producer

Writer/s

Actors

Reaction/Review/ Plot/Quotes/

Who I saw it with: Cost:

                                                               £

Theatre

☆ ☆ ☆ ☆ ☆

Title   Year

Director   Producer

Writer/s

Actors

Reaction/Review/ Plot/Quotes/

Who I saw it with: Cost:

£

Theatre

☆ ☆ ☆ ☆ ☆

Title

Year

Director

Producer

Writer/s

Actors

Reaction/Review/ Plot/Quotes/

Who I saw it with:

Cost:

£

Theatre

☆ ☆ ☆ ☆ ☆

Title   Year

Director   Producer

Writer/s

Actors

Reaction/Review/ Plot/Quotes/

Who I saw it with: Cost:

£

Theatre

☆ ☆ ☆ ☆ ☆

Title

Year

Director

Producer

Writer/s

Actors

Reaction/Review/ Plot/Quotes/

Who I saw it with:

Cost:

£

Theatre

☆ ☆ ☆ ☆ ☆

Title   Year

Director   Producer

Writer/s

Actors

Reaction/Review/ Plot/Quotes/

Who I saw it with: Cost:

                                                                         £

Theatre

☆ ☆ ☆ ☆ ☆

Title   Year

Director   Producer

Writer/s

Actors

Reaction/Review/ Plot/Quotes/

Who I saw it with: Cost:

£

Theatre

☆ ☆ ☆ ☆ ☆

Title

Year

Director

Producer

Writer/s

Actors

Reaction/Review/ Plot/Quotes/

Who I saw it with:

Cost:

£

Theatre

☆ ☆ ☆ ☆ ☆

Title Year

Director Producer

Writer/s

Actors

Reaction/Review/ Plot/Quotes/

Who I saw it with: Cost:

£

Theatre

☆ ☆ ☆ ☆ ☆

Title

Year

Director

Producer

Writer/s

Actors

Reaction/Review/ Plot/Quotes/

Who I saw it with:

Cost:

£

Theatre

☆ ☆ ☆ ☆ ☆

Title

Year

Director

Producer

Writer/s

Actors

Reaction/Review/ Plot/Quotes/

Who 9 saw it with:

Cost:

£

Theatre

☆ ☆ ☆ ☆ ☆

Title   Year

Director   Producer

Writer/s

Actors

Reaction/Review/ Plot/Quotes/

Who I saw it with: Cost:

£

Theatre

☆ ☆ ☆ ☆ ☆

Title

Year

Director

Producer

Writer/s

Actors

Reaction/Review/ Plot/Quotes/

Who I saw it with:

Cost:

£

Theatre

☆ ☆ ☆ ☆ ☆

Title

Year

Director

Producer

Writer/s

Actors

Reaction/Review/ Plot/Quotes/

Who I saw it with:

Cost:

£

Theatre

☆ ☆ ☆ ☆ ☆

Title   Year

Director   Producer

Writer/s

Actors

Reaction/Review/ Plot/Quotes/

Who I saw it with: Cost:

                                                         £

Theatre

☆ ☆ ☆ ☆ ☆

Title

Year

Director

Producer

Writer/s

Actors

Reaction/Review/ Plot/Quotes/

Who I saw it with:

Cost:

£

Theatre

☆ ☆ ☆ ☆ ☆

Title   Year

Director   Producer

Writer/s

Actors

Reaction/Review/ Plot/Quotes/

Who I saw it with: Cost:

£

Theatre

☆ ☆ ☆ ☆ ☆

Title   Year

Director   Producer

Writer/s

Actors

Reaction/Review/ Plot/Quotes/

Who I saw it with: Cost:

                                                         £

Theatre

☆ ☆ ☆ ☆ ☆

Title

Year

Director

Producer

Writer/s

Actors

Reaction/Review/ Plot/Quotes/

Who I saw it with:

Cost:

£

Theatre

☆ ☆ ☆ ☆ ☆

Title

Year

Director

Producer

Writer/s

Actors

Reaction/Review/ Plot/Quotes/

Who I saw it with:

Cost:

£

Theatre

☆ ☆ ☆ ☆ ☆

Title   Year

Director   Producer

Writer/s

Actors

Reaction/Review/ Plot/Quotes/

Who I saw it with: Cost:

£

Theatre

☆ ☆ ☆ ☆ ☆

Title   Year

Director   Producer

Writer/s

Actors

Reaction/Review/ Plot/Quotes/

Who I saw it with: Cost:

£

Theatre

☆ ☆ ☆ ☆ ☆

Title

Year

Director

Producer

Writer/s

Actors

Reaction/Review/ Plot/Quotes/

Who I saw it with:

Cost:

£

Theatre

☆ ☆ ☆ ☆ ☆

Title   Year

Director   Producer

Writer/s

Actors

Reaction/Review/ Plot/Quotes/

Who I saw it with: Cost:

£

Theatre

☆ ☆ ☆ ☆ ☆

Title

Year

Director

Producer

Writer/s

Actors

Reaction/Review/ Plot/Quotes/

Who 9 saw it with:

Cost:

£

Theatre

☆ ☆ ☆ ☆ ☆

Title

Year

Director

Producer

Writer/s

Actors

Reaction/Review/ Plot/Quotes/

Who I saw it with:

Cost:

£

Theatre

☆ ☆ ☆ ☆ ☆

Title

Year

Director

Producer

Writer/s

Actors

Reaction/Review/ Plot/Quotes/

Who 9 saw it with:

Cost:

£

Theatre

☆ ☆ ☆ ☆ ☆

Title   Year

Director   Producer

Writer/s

Actors

Reaction/Review/ Plot/Quotes/

Who I saw it with: Cost:

£

Theatre

☆ ☆ ☆ ☆ ☆

Title   Year

Director   Producer

Writer/s

Actors

Reaction/Review/ Plot/Quotes/

Who I saw it with: Cost:

£

Theatre

☆ ☆ ☆ ☆ ☆

Title

Year

Director

Producer

Writer/s

Actors

.

Reaction/Review/ Plot/Quotes/

Who I saw it with:

Cost:

£

Theatre

☆ ☆ ☆ ☆ ☆

Title   Year

Director   Producer

Writer/s

Actors

Reaction/Review/ Plot/Quotes/

Who I saw it with: Cost:

                                                           £

Theatre

☆ ☆ ☆ ☆ ☆

Title   Year

Director   Producer

Writer/s

Actors

Reaction/Review/ Plot/Quotes/

Who I saw it with: Cost:

                                                         £

Theatre

☆ ☆ ☆ ☆ ☆

Title   Year

Director   Producer

Writer/s

Actors

Reaction/Review/ Plot/Quotes/

Who I saw it with: Cost:

£

Theatre

☆ ☆ ☆ ☆ ☆

Title

Year

Director

Producer

Writer/s

Actors

Reaction/Review/ Plot/Quotes/

Who 9 saw it with:

Cost:

£

Theatre

☆ ☆ ☆ ☆ ☆

Title

Year

Director

Producer

Writer/s

Actors

Reaction/Review/ Plot/Quotes/

Who 9 saw it with:

Cost:

£

Theatre

☆ ☆ ☆ ☆ ☆

Title   Year

Director   Producer

Writer/s

Actors

Reaction/Review/ Plot/Quotes/

Who 9 saw it with: Cost:

£

Theatre

☆ ☆ ☆ ☆ ☆

Title   Year

Director   Producer

Writer/s

Actors

Reaction/Review/ Plot/Quotes/

Who I saw it with: Cost:

                                                                         £

Theatre

☆ ☆ ☆ ☆ ☆

Title

Year

Director

Producer

Writer/s

Actors

Reaction/Review/ Plot/Quotes/

Who I saw it with:

Cost:

£

Theatre

☆ ☆ ☆ ☆ ☆

Title

Year

Director

Producer

Writer/s

Actors

Reaction/Review/ Plot/Quotes/

Who I saw it with:

Cost:

£

Theatre

☆ ☆ ☆ ☆ ☆

Title   Year

Director   Producer

Writer/s

Actors

Reaction/Review/ Plot/Quotes/

Who I saw it with: Cost:

                                                               £

Theatre

☆ ☆ ☆ ☆ ☆

Title   Year

Director   Producer

Writer/s

Actors

Reaction/Review/ Plot/Quotes/

Who I saw it with: Cost:

                                                         £

Theatre

☆ ☆ ☆ ☆ ☆

Title   Year

Director   Producer

Writer/s

Actors

Reaction/Review/ Plot/Quotes/

Who 9 saw it with: Cost:

£

Theatre

☆ ☆ ☆ ☆ ☆

Title

Year

Director

Producer

Writer/s

Actors

Reaction/Review/ Plot/Quotes/

Who 9 saw it with:

Cost:

£

Theatre

☆ ☆ ☆ ☆ ☆

Title

Year

Director

Producer

Writer/s

Actors

Reaction/Review/ Plot/Quotes/

Who 9 saw it with:

Cost:

£

Theatre

☆ ☆ ☆ ☆ ☆

Title

Year

Director

Producer

Writer/s

Actors

Reaction/Review/ Plot/Quotes/

Who I saw it with:

Cost:

£

Theatre

☆ ☆ ☆ ☆ ☆

Title

Year

Director

Producer

Writer/s

Actors

Reaction/Review/ Plot/Quotes/

Who I saw it with:

Cost:

£

Theatre

☆ ☆ ☆ ☆ ☆

Title   Year

Director   Producer

Writer/s

Actors

Reaction/Review/ Plot/Quotes/

Who 9 saw it with: Cost:

                                                         £
Theatre

☆ ☆ ☆ ☆ ☆

Title   Year

Director   Producer

Writer/s

Actors

Reaction/Review/ Plot/Quotes/

Who I saw it with: Cost:

£

Theatre

☆ ☆ ☆ ☆ ☆

Title

Year

Director

Producer

Writer/s

Actors

Reaction/Review/ Plot/Quotes/

Who I saw it with:

Cost:

£

Theatre

☆ ☆ ☆ ☆ ☆

Title

Year

Director

Producer

Writer/s

Actors

Reaction/Review/ Plot/Quotes/

Who 9 saw it with:

Cost:

£

Theatre

☆ ☆ ☆ ☆ ☆

Title

Year

Director

Producer

Writer/s

Actors

Reaction/Review/ Plot/Quotes/

Who I saw it with:

Cost:

£

Theatre

☆ ☆ ☆ ☆ ☆

Title   Year

Director   Producer

Writer/s

Actors

Reaction/Review/ Plot/Quotes/

Who I saw it with: Cost:

                                                                   £

Theatre

☆ ☆ ☆ ☆ ☆

Title   Year

Director   Producer

Writer/s

Actors

Reaction/Review/ Plot/Quotes/

Who 9 saw it with: Cost:

£

Theatre

☆ ☆ ☆ ☆ ☆

Title
Year

Director
Producer

Writer/s

Actors

Reaction/Review/ Plot/Quotes/

Who I saw it with:
Cost:

£

Theatre

☆ ☆ ☆ ☆ ☆

Title

Year

Director

Producer

Writer/s

Actors

Reaction/Review/ Plot/Quotes/

Who I saw it with:

Cost:

£

Theatre

☆ ☆ ☆ ☆ ☆

Title

Year

Director

Producer

Writer/s

Actors

Reaction/Review/ Plot/Quotes/

Who I saw it with:

Cost:

£

Theatre

☆ ☆ ☆ ☆ ☆

Title

Year

Director

Producer

Writer/s

Actors

Reaction/Review/ Plot/Quotes/

Who 9 saw it with:

Cost:

£

Theatre

☆ ☆ ☆ ☆ ☆

Title   Year

Director   Producer

Writer/s

Actors

Reaction/Review/ Plot/Quotes/

Who I saw it with: Cost:

                                                               £

Theatre

☆ ☆ ☆ ☆ ☆

Title   Year

Director   Producer

Writer/s

Actors

Reaction/Review/ Plot/Quotes/

Who I saw it with: Cost:

                                                                £

Theatre

☆ ☆ ☆ ☆ ☆

Title

Year

Director

Producer

Writer/s

Actors

Reaction/Review/ Plot/Quotes/

Who 9 saw it with:

Cost:

£

Theatre

☆ ☆ ☆ ☆ ☆

Title

Year

Director

Producer

Writer/s

Actors

Reaction/Review/ Plot/Quotes/

Who I saw it with:

Cost:

£

Theatre

☆ ☆ ☆ ☆ ☆

Title   Year

Director   Producer

Writer/s

Actors

Reaction/Review/ Plot/Quotes/

Who I saw it with: Cost:

                                                               £

Theatre

☆ ☆ ☆ ☆ ☆

Title

Year

Director

Producer

Writer/s

Actors

Reaction/Review/ Plot/Quotes/

Who I saw it with:

Cost:

£

Theatre

☆ ☆ ☆ ☆ ☆

Title   Year

Director   Producer

Writer/s

Actors

Reaction/Review/ Plot/Quotes/

Who I saw it with: Cost:

£

Theatre

☆ ☆ ☆ ☆ ☆

Title

Year

Director

Producer

Writer/s

Actors

Reaction/Review/ Plot/Quotes/

Who 9 saw it with:

Cost:

£

Theatre

☆ ☆ ☆ ☆ ☆

Title _____ Year _____

Director _____ Producer _____

Writer/s _____

Actors _____

Reaction/Review/ Plot/Quotes/ _____

Who I saw it with: _____ Cost:

£ _____

Theatre _____

☆ ☆ ☆ ☆ ☆

Title

Year

Director

Producer

Writer/s

Actors

Reaction/Review/ Plot/Quotes/

Who I saw it with:

Cost:

£

Theatre

☆ ☆ ☆ ☆ ☆

Title

Year

Director

Producer

Writer/s

Actors

Reaction/Review/ Plot/Quotes/

Who I saw it with:

Cost:

£

Theatre

☆ ☆ ☆ ☆ ☆

Title   Year

Director   Producer

Writer/s

Actors

Reaction/Review/ Plot/Quotes/

Who I saw it with: Cost:

                                                              £

Theatre

☆ ☆ ☆ ☆ ☆

Title

Year

Director

Producer

Writer/s

Actors

Reaction/Review/ Plot/Quotes/

Who I saw it with:

Cost:

£

Theatre

☆ ☆ ☆ ☆ ☆

Title   Year

Director   Producer

Writer/s

Actors

Reaction/Review/ Plot/Quotes/

Who I saw it with: Cost:

£

Theatre

☆ ☆ ☆ ☆ ☆

Title

Year

Director

Producer

Writer/s

Actors

Reaction/Review/ Plot/Quotes/

Who I saw it with:

Cost:

£

Theatre

☆ ☆ ☆ ☆ ☆

Title

Year

Director

Producer

Writer/s

Actors

Reaction/Review/ Plot/Quotes/

Who I saw it with:

Cost:

£

Theatre

☆ ☆ ☆ ☆ ☆

Title   Year

Director   Producer

Writer/s

Actors

Reaction/Review/ Plot/Quotes/

Who I saw it with: Cost:

£

Theatre

☆ ☆ ☆ ☆ ☆

Title   Year

Director   Producer

Writer/s

Actors

Reaction/Review/ Plot/Quotes/

Who I saw it with: Cost:

                                                         £

Theatre

☆ ☆ ☆ ☆ ☆

Title

Year

Director

Producer

Writer/s

Actors

Reaction/Review/ Plot/Quotes/

Who I saw it with:

Cost:

£

Theatre

☆ ☆ ☆ ☆ ☆

Title   Year

Director   Producer

Writer/s

Actors

Reaction/Review/ Plot/Quotes/

Who I saw it with: Cost:

                                                           £
Theatre

☆ ☆ ☆ ☆ ☆

Title

Year

Director

Producer

Writer/s

Actors

Reaction/Review/ Plot/Quotes/

Who I saw it with:

Cost:

£

Theatre

☆ ☆ ☆ ☆ ☆

Title

Year

Director

Producer

Writer/s

Actors

Reaction/Review/ Plot/Quotes/

Who 9 saw it with:

Cost:

£

Theatre

☆ ☆ ☆ ☆ ☆

Title

Year

Director

Producer

Writer/s

Actors

Reaction/Review/ Plot/Quotes/

Who I saw it with:

Cost:

£

Theatre

☆ ☆ ☆ ☆ ☆

Title

Year

Director

Producer

Writer/s

Actors

Reaction/Review/ Plot/Quotes/

Who I saw it with:

Cost:

£

Theatre

☆ ☆ ☆ ☆ ☆

Title

Year

Director

Producer

Writer/s

Actors

Reaction/Review/ Plot/Quotes/

Who I saw it with:

Cost:

£

Theatre

☆ ☆ ☆ ☆ ☆

Title   Year

Director   Producer

Writer/s

Actors

Reaction/Review/ Plot/Quotes/

Who I saw it with: Cost:

                                                           £

Theatre

☆ ☆ ☆ ☆ ☆

Title

Year

Director

Producer

Writer/s

Actors

Reaction/Review/ Plot/Quotes/

Who I saw it with:

Cost:

£

Theatre

☆ ☆ ☆ ☆ ☆

Title

Year

Director

Producer

Writer/s

Actors

Reaction/Review/ Plot/Quotes/

Who I saw it with:

Cost:

£

Theatre

☆ ☆ ☆ ☆ ☆

Title   Year

Director   Producer

Writer/s

Actors

Reaction/Review/ Plot/Quotes/

Who I saw it with: Cost:

                                                               £

Theatre

☆ ☆ ☆ ☆ ☆

Title   Year

Director   Producer

Writer/s

Actors

Reaction/Review/ Plot/Quotes/

Who I saw it with: Cost:

£

Theatre

☆ ☆ ☆ ☆ ☆

Title

Year

Director

Producer

Writer/s

Actors

Reaction/Review/ Plot/Quotes/

Who I saw it with:

Cost:

£

Theatre

☆ ☆ ☆ ☆ ☆

Title

Year

Director

Producer

Writer/s

Actors

Reaction/Review/ Plot/Quotes/

Who I saw it with:

Cost:

£

Theatre

☆ ☆ ☆ ☆ ☆

Title   Year

Director   Producer

Writer/s

Actors

Reaction/Review/ Plot/Quotes/

Who I saw it with: Cost:

                                                         £

Theatre

☆ ☆ ☆ ☆ ☆

Title

Year

Director

Producer

Writer/s

Actors

Reaction/Review/ Plot/Quotes/

Who I saw it with:

Cost:

£

Theatre

☆ ☆ ☆ ☆ ☆

Title

Year

Director

Producer

Writer/s

Actors

Reaction/Review/ Plot/Quotes/

Who I saw it with:

Cost:

£

Theatre

☆ ☆ ☆ ☆ ☆

Title   Year

Director   Producer

Writer/s

Actors

Reaction/Review/ Plot/Quotes/

Who I saw it with: Cost:

                                               £

Theatre

☆ ☆ ☆ ☆ ☆

Title

Year

Director

Producer

Writer/s

Actors

Reaction/Review/ Plot/Quotes/

Who 9 saw it with:

Cost:

£

Theatre

☆ ☆ ☆ ☆ ☆

Title

Year

Director

Producer

Writer/s

Actors

Reaction/Review/ Plot/Quotes/

Who I saw it with:

Cost:

£

Theatre

☆ ☆ ☆ ☆ ☆

Title

Year

Director

Producer

Writer/s

Actors

Reaction/Review/ Plot/Quotes/

Who I saw it with:

Cost:

£

Theatre

☆ ☆ ☆ ☆ ☆

Title

Year

Director

Producer

Writer/s

Actors

Reaction/Review/ Plot/Quotes/

Who I saw it with:

Cost:

£

Theatre

☆ ☆ ☆ ☆ ☆

Title

Year

Director

Producer

Writer/s

Actors

Reaction/Review/ Plot/Quotes/

Who I saw it with:

Cost:

£

Theatre

☆ ☆ ☆ ☆ ☆

Title   Year

Director   Producer

Writer/s

Actors

Reaction/Review/ Plot/Quotes/

Who I saw it with: Cost:

                                                                      £

Theatre

☆ ☆ ☆ ☆ ☆

Title   Year

Director   Producer

Writer/s

Actors

Reaction/Review/ Plot/Quotes/

Who I saw it with: Cost:

                                                      £

Theatre

☆ ☆ ☆ ☆ ☆

Title   Year

Director   Producer

Writer/s

Actors

Reaction/Review/ Plot/Quotes/

Who I saw it with: Cost:

                                                               £

Theatre

☆ ☆ ☆ ☆ ☆

Title

Year

Director

Producer

Writer/s

Actors

Reaction/Review/ Plot/Quotes/

Who I saw it with:

Cost:

£

Theatre

☆ ☆ ☆ ☆ ☆

Title   Year

Director   Producer

Writer/s

Actors

Reaction/Review/ Plot/Quotes/

Who I saw it with: Cost:

                                         £

Theatre

☆ ☆ ☆ ☆ ☆

Title   Year

Director   Producer

Writer/s

Actors

Reaction/Review/ Plot/Quotes/

Who I saw it with: Cost:

                                                                                   £

Theatre

☆ ☆ ☆ ☆ ☆

Title

Year

Director

Producer

Writer/s

Actors

Reaction/Review/ Plot/Quotes/

Who I saw it with:

Cost:

£

Theatre

☆ ☆ ☆ ☆ ☆

Title

Year

Director

Producer

Writer/s

Actors

Reaction/Review/ Plot/Quotes/

Who I saw it with:

Cost:

£

Theatre

☆ ☆ ☆ ☆ ☆

Title   Year

Director   Producer

Writer/s

Actors

Reaction/Review/ Plot/Quotes/

Who I saw it with: Cost:

£

Theatre

☆ ☆ ☆ ☆ ☆

Title   Year

Director   Producer

Writer/s

Actors

Reaction/Review/ Plot/Quotes/

Who I saw it with: Cost:

                                                         £

Theatre

☆ ☆ ☆ ☆ ☆

Title   Year

Director   Producer

Writer/s

Actors

Reaction/Review/ Plot/Quotes/

Who I saw it with: Cost:

                                                              £

Theatre

☆ ☆ ☆ ☆ ☆

Title

Year

Director

Producer

Writer/s

Actors

Reaction/Review/ Plot/Quotes/

Who I saw it with:

Cost:

£

Theatre

☆ ☆ ☆ ☆ ☆

Title

Year

Director

Producer

Writer/s

Actors

Reaction/Review/ Plot/Quotes/

Who I saw it with:

Cost:

£

Theatre

☆ ☆ ☆ ☆ ☆

Title   Year

Director   Producer

Writer/s

Actors

Reaction/Review/ Plot/Quotes/

Who I saw it with: Cost:

£

Theatre

☆ ☆ ☆ ☆ ☆

Title

Year

Director

Producer

Writer/s

Actors

Reaction/Review/ Plot/Quotes/

Who I saw it with:

Cost:

£

Theatre

☆ ☆ ☆ ☆ ☆

Title

Year

Director

Producer

Writer/s

Actors

Reaction/Review/ Plot/Quotes/

Who I saw it with:

Cost:

£

Theatre

☆ ☆ ☆ ☆ ☆

Title

Year

Director

Producer

Writer/s

Actors

Reaction/Review/ Plot/Quotes/

Who I saw it with:

Cost:

£

Theatre

☆ ☆ ☆ ☆ ☆

Title

Year

Director

Producer

Writer/s

Actors

Reaction/Review/ Plot/Quotes/

Who I saw it with:

Cost:

£

Theatre

☆ ☆ ☆ ☆ ☆

Title

Year

Director

Producer

Writer/s

Actors

Reaction/Review/ Plot/Quotes/

Who I saw it with:

Cost:

£

Theatre

☆ ☆ ☆ ☆ ☆

Title   Year

Director   Producer

Writer/s

Actors

Reaction/Review/ Plot/Quotes/

Who I saw it with: Cost:

                                                            £

Theatre

Title   Year

Director   Producer

Writer/s

Actors

Reaction/Review/ Plot/Quotes/

Who I saw it with: Cost:

£

Theatre

☆ ☆ ☆ ☆ ☆

Title

Year

Director

Producer

Writer/s

Actors

Reaction/Review/ Plot/Quotes/

Who I saw it with:

Cost:

£

Theatre

☆ ☆ ☆ ☆ ☆

Title

Year

Director

Producer

Writer/s

Actors

Reaction/Review/ Plot/Quotes/

Who I saw it with:

Cost:

£

Theatre

☆ ☆ ☆ ☆ ☆

Title

Year

Director

Producer

Writer/s

Actors

Reaction/Review/ Plot/Quotes/

Who I saw it with:

Cost:

£

Theatre

☆ ☆ ☆ ☆ ☆

Title

Year

Director

Producer

Writer/s

Actors

Reaction/Review/ Plot/Quotes/

Who I saw it with:

Cost:

£

Theatre

☆ ☆ ☆ ☆ ☆

Title

Year

Director

Producer

Writer/s

Actors

Reaction/Review/ Plot/Quotes/

Who I saw it with:

Cost:

£

Theatre

☆ ☆ ☆ ☆ ☆

Title

Year

Director

Producer

Writer/s

Actors

Reaction/Review/ Plot/Quotes/

Who I saw it with:

Cost:

£

Theatre

☆ ☆ ☆ ☆ ☆

Title

Year

Director

Producer

Writer/s

Actors

Reaction/Review/ Plot/Quotes/

Who I saw it with:

Cost:

£

Theatre

Title

Year

Director

Producer

Writer/s

Actors

Reaction/Review/ Plot/Quotes/

Who I saw it with:

Cost:

£

Theatre

☆ ☆ ☆ ☆ ☆

Title   Year

Director   Producer

Writer/s

Actors

Reaction/Review/ Plot/Quotes/

Who I saw it with: Cost:

£

Theatre

☆ ☆ ☆ ☆ ☆

Title   Year

Director   Producer

Writer/s

Actors

Reaction/Review/ Plot/Quotes/

Who I saw it with: Cost:

                                                     £

Theatre

☆ ☆ ☆ ☆ ☆

Title   Year

Director   Producer

Writer/s

Actors

Reaction/Review/ Plot/Quotes/

Who I saw it with: Cost:

                                                                          £

Theatre

☆ ☆ ☆ ☆ ☆

Title

Year

Director

Producer

Writer/s

Actors

Reaction/Review/ Plot/Quotes/

Who I saw it with:

Cost:

£

Theatre

☆ ☆ ☆ ☆ ☆

Title

Year

Director

Producer

Writer/s

Actors

Reaction/Review/ Plot/Quotes/

Who I saw it with:

Cost:

£

Theatre

☆ ☆ ☆ ☆ ☆

Title   Year

Director   Producer

Writer/s

Actors

Reaction/Review/ Plot/Quotes/

Who I saw it with: Cost:

                                               £

Theatre

☆ ☆ ☆ ☆ ☆

Title

Year

Director

Producer

Writer/s

Actors

Reaction/Review/ Plot/Quotes/

Who I saw it with:

Cost:

£

Theatre

☆ ☆ ☆ ☆ ☆

Title

Year

Director

Producer

Writer/s

Actors

Reaction/Review/ Plot/Quotes/

Who I saw it with:

Cost:

£

Theatre

☆ ☆ ☆ ☆ ☆

Title

Year

Director

Producer

Writer/s

Actors

Reaction/Review/ Plot/Quotes/

Who I saw it with:

Cost:

£

Theatre

☆ ☆ ☆ ☆ ☆

Title

Year

Director

Producer

Writer/s

Actors

Reaction/Review/ Plot/Quotes/

Who 9 saw it with:

Cost:

£

Theatre

☆ ☆ ☆ ☆ ☆

Title

Year

Director

Producer

Writer/s

Actors

Reaction/Review/ Plot/Quotes/

Who I saw it with:

Cost:

£

Theatre

☆ ☆ ☆ ☆ ☆

Title

Year

Director

Producer

Writer/s

Actors

Reaction/Review/ Plot/Quotes/

Who I saw it with:

Cost:

£

Theatre

☆ ☆ ☆ ☆ ☆

Favorite Plays

Title: Year:

Director: Genre

Writer:

Actors:

Title: Year:

Director: Genre

Writer/s:

Actors:

Title: Year:

Director: Genre

Writer/s:

Actors:

Title: Year:

Director: Genre

Writer/s:

Actors:

Favorite Plays

Title: _____ Year: _____

Director: _____ Genre _____

Writer: _____

Actors: _____

Title: _____ Year: _____

Director: _____ Genre _____

Writer/s: _____

Actors: _____

Title: _____ Year: _____

Director: _____ Genre _____

Writer/s: _____

Actors: _____

Title: _____ Year: _____

Director: _____ Genre _____

Writer/s: _____

Actors: _____

Favorite Plays

Title: _____ Year: _____

Director: _____ Genre _____

Writer: _____

Actors: _____

Title: _____ Year: _____

Director: _____ Genre _____

Writer/s: _____

Actors: _____

Title: _____ Year: _____

Director: _____ Genre _____

Writer/s: _____

Actors: _____

Title: _____ Year: _____

Director: _____ Genre _____

Writer/s: _____

Actors: _____

Favorite Actors

Name   D.O.B. / /

Bio:

Theatrical Productions:

Name   D.O.B. / /

Bio:

Theatrical Productions:

Favorite Actors

Name _____ D.O.B. / /

Bio:

_____

Theatrical Productions:

_____

Name _____ D.O.B. / /

Bio:

_____

Theatrical Productions:

_____

Favorite Actors

Name   D.O.B. / /

Bio:

Theatrical Productions:

Name   D.O.B. / /

Bio:

Theatrical Productions:

Favorite Actors

Name   D.O.B. / /

Bio:

Theatrical Productions:

Name   D.O.B. / /

Bio:

Theatrical Productions:

Favorite Actors

Name   D.O.B. / /

Bio:

Theatrical Productions:

Name   D.O.B. / /

Bio:

Theatrical Productions:

Favorite Directors

Name _____ D.O.B. / /

Bio:

Theatrical Productions:

Name _____ D.O.B. / /

Bio:

Theatrical Productions:

Favorite Directors

Name _____ D.O.B. __/__/__

Bio:

Theatrical Productions:

Name _____ D.O.B. __/__/__

Bio:

Theatrical Productions:

Favorite Directors

Name   D.O.B. / /

Bio:

Theatrical Productions:

Name   D.O.B. / /

Bio:

Theatrical Productions:

Favorite Producers

Name _____ D.O.B. _ / _ / _

Bio:

Theatrical Productions:

Name _____ D.O.B. _ / _ / _

Bio:

Theatrical Productions:

Favorite Producers

Name   D.O.B. / /
Bio:

Theatrical Productions:

Name   D.O.B. / /
Bio:

Theatrical Productions:

Favorite Writers

Name _____ D.O.B. / /

Bio:

Theatrical Productions:

Name _____ D.O.B. / /

Bio:

Theatrical Productions:

Favorite Writers

Name _____ D.O.B. / /
Bio:

_____

Theatrical Productions:

_____

Name _____ D.O.B. / /
Bio:

_____

Theatrical Productions:

_____

Favorite Writers

Name   D.O.B.   /   /

Bio:

Theatrical Productions:

Name   D.O.B.   /   /

Bio:

Theatrical Productions:

Wisk List		
Theatrical Productions	Details	Date

Wisk List		
Theatrical Productions	Details	Date

Notes:

Printed in Great Britain
by Amazon